How Competition Makes You A Better Product Manager

How Product Managers Can Use
Challenges To Advance Their Careers

"Practical, proven examples of how successful
product managers approach competition!"

Dr. Jim Anderson

Published by:
Blue Elephant Consulting
Tampa, Florida

Printed in the United States of America

Library of Congress Control Number: 2014952843

ISBN-13: 978-1502562050
ISBN-10: 1502562057

Warning – Disclaimer

The purpose of this book is to educate and entertain. This book does not promise or guarantee that anyone following the ideas, tips, suggestions, techniques or strategies will be successful. The author, publisher and distributor(s) shall have neither liability nor responsibility to anyone with respect to any loss or damage caused, or alleged to be caused, directly or indirectly by the information contained in this book.

Recent Books By The Author

Product Management

- How Product Managers Can Grow Their Career: How Product Managers Can Find And Succeed In The Right Job

- Sales Secrets For Product Managers: Tips & Techniques For Product Managers To Better Understand How To Sell Their Product

Public Speaking

- How To Become A Better Speaker By Changing How You Speak: Change techniques that will transform a speech into a memorable event

- How To Give A Great Presentation: Presentation techniques that will transform a speech into a memorable event

CIO Skills

- How CIOs Can Solve The Security Puzzle: Tips And Techniques For CIOs To Use In Order To Secure Both Their IT Department And Their Company

- What CIOs Need To Know About Working With Partners: Techniques For CIOs To Use In Order To Be Able To Successfully Work With Partners

IT Manager Skills

- Team Building Strategies For IT Managers: Tips And Techniques That IT Managers Can Use In Order To Develop Productive Teams

- Secrets Of Effective Leadership For IT Managers: Tips And Techniques That IT Managers Can Use In Order To Develop Leadership Skills

Negotiating

- Learn How To Package Trades In Your Next Negotiation: How To Develop The Skill Of Assembling Potential Trades In Order To Get The Best Possible Outcome

- Learn How To Signal In Your Next Negotiation: How To Develop The Skill Of Effective Signaling In A Negotiation In Order To Get The Best Possible Outcome

Miscellaneous

- Power Distribution Unit (PDU) Secrets: What Everyone Who Works In A Data Center Needs To Know!

- Making The Jump: How To Land Your Dream Job When You Get Out Of College!

Note: See a complete list of books by Dr. Jim Anderson at the back of this book.

Acknowledgements

Any book like this one is the result of years of real-world work experience. In my over 25 years of working for 7 different firms, I have met countless fantastic people and I've been mentored by some truly exceptional ones. Although I've probably forgotten some of the people who made me the person that I am today, here is my attempt to finally give them the recognition that they so truly deserve:

- Thomas P. Anderson
- Art Puett
- Bobbi Marshall
- Bob Boggs

Dr. Jim Anderson

This book is dedicated to my family: Lori, Maddie, Nick, and Ben. None of this would have been possible without their constant love and support.

Thanks for always believing in me and providing me with the strength to always be willing to go out there and be my best for you.

Speaking.   Negotiating.   Managing.   Marketing.

Table Of Contents

It's Competition That Pushes Us Forward

As product managers, we all want to become better at what we do. However, sometimes we can find ourselves in a rut: we've solved the immediate problems, our product is doing well, and we've just lost that drive that we need in order to reach the next level.

This is when the power of competition comes in. We all like a good challenge. When we are faced with a situation in which we might not be the best, or we might not know exactly what we should do, that's when we can become our best.

Competitive situations for product managers can take on a number of different forms. They can be as simple as placing ourselves into a setting in which we are called on to network with others. Maybe it's as simple as challenging us to pay closer attention to what's going on – easy to say, hard to do.

Mastering competition requires us to become experts at a lot of different skills. These include managing other people, finding mentors, and continuing our education. Throw in things like learning to stop multitasking and how to create an effective resume and all of a sudden you have some fairly challenging tasks ahead of you.

The good news is that every product manager can rise to meet these challenges. No matter if it's learning how to find your next product manager job or how to deal with a situation in which you've been passed over for a promised promotion, your ability to deal with the competition that comes along with your product manager job will be the key to your long term success.

For more information on what it takes to be a great product manager, check out my blog, The Accidental Product Manager, at:

www.TheAccidentalPM.com

Good luck!

- Dr. Jim Anderson

About The Author

I must confess that I never set out to be a product manager. When I went to school, I studied Computer Science and thought that I'd get a nice job programming and that would be that. Well, at least part of that plan worked out!

My first job was working for Boeing on their F/A-18 fighter jet program. I spent my days programming fighter jet software in assembly language and I loved it. The U.S. government decided to save some money and went looking for other countries to sell this plane to. This put me into an unfamiliar role: I started to meet with foreign military officials in order to explain what my product did.

Time moved on and so did I. I found myself working for Siemens, the big German telecommunications company. They were making phone switches and selling them to the seven U.S. phone companies. The problem was that the switches were too complicated. Customers couldn't tell the difference between one complicated phone switch from another complicated phone switch.

The Siemens sales folks were in a bind. They didn't know enough about how the switches worked to tell their customers why they should buy them. Siemens reached out into their engineering unit looking for anyone who could help the sales teams out. I put my hand up and overnight I became a product manager.

Since then I've spent over 20 years working as a product manager for both big companies and startups. This has given me an opportunity to do everything that a product manager does many, many times. I know what works as well as what doesn't work.

I now live in Tampa Florida where I spend my time managing my consulting business, Blue Elephant Consulting, teaching college courses at the University of South Florida, and traveling to work with companies like yours to share the knowledge that I have about how product managers can make their product be a success.

I'm always available to answer questions and I can be reached at:

Dr. Jim Anderson
Blue Elephant Consulting
Email: jim@BlueElephantConsulting.com
Facebook: http://goo.gl/1TVoK
Web: **www.BlueElephantConsulting.com**

"Unforgettable communication skills that will set your ideas free..."

Create Products Your Customers Want At A Price That They Are Willing To Pay!

Dr. Jim Anderson is available to provide training and coaching on the two topics that are the most important to product managers everywhere: how do I create the products that my customers want and what should I price them at?

Dr. Anderson believes that in order to both learn and remember what he says, product managers need to laugh. Each one of his speeches is full of fun and humor so that what he says "sticks" with everyone.

Dr. Anderson's Product Management Training Includes:

1. How can you segment your market?
2. What problems are your customers having right now?
3. Which of your customer's problems does your product solve?
4. How much of this problem does your product solve?
5. How much will it cost your customer if they don't fix this problem?

Dr. Jim Anderson presents over 100 speeches per year. To invite Dr. Anderson to speak at your event, contact him at:

Phone: 813-418-6970 or
Email: jim@BlueElephantConsulting.com

Blue
Elephant
Consulting

Speaking. Negotiating. Managing. Marketing.

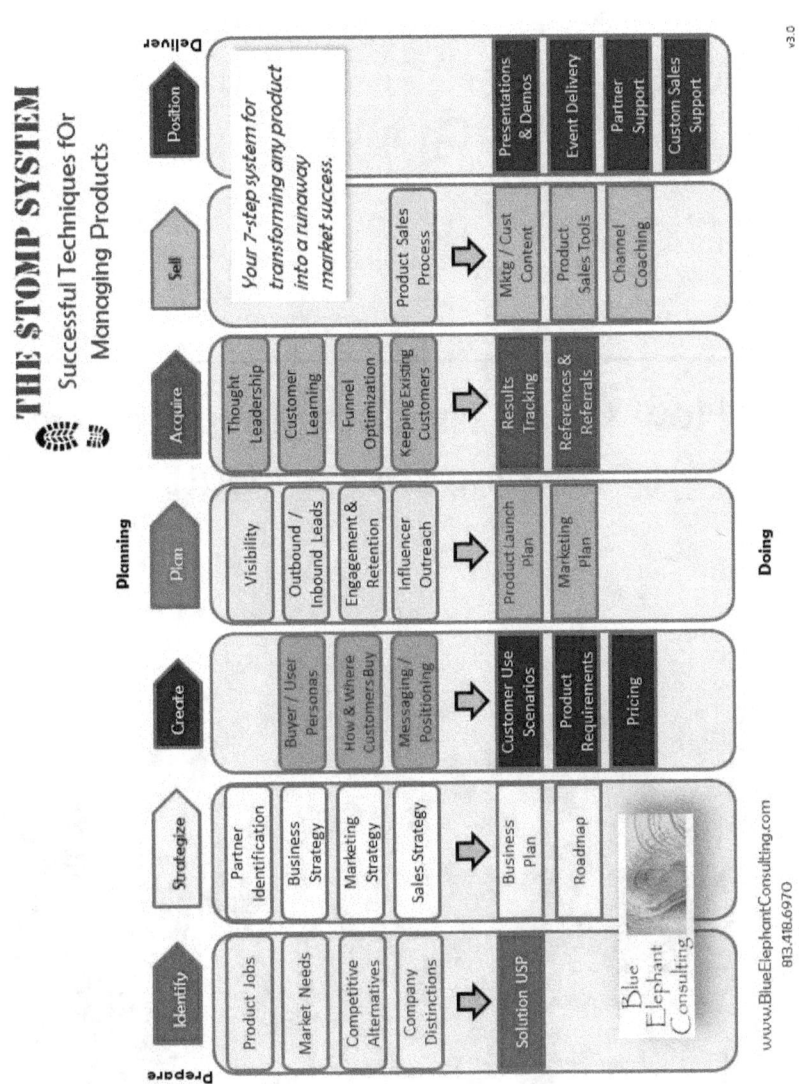

THE $TOMP SYSTEM
Successful Techniques fOr Managing Products

Identify — Product Jobs, Market Needs, Competitive Alternatives, Company Distinctions → Solution USP

Strategize — Partner Identification, Business Strategy, Marketing Strategy, Sales Strategy → Business Plan, Roadmap

Create — Buyer / User Personas, How & Where Customers Buy, Messaging / Positioning → Customer Use Scenarios, Product Requirements, Pricing

Plan — Visibility, Outbound / Inbound Leads, Engagement & Retention, Influencer Outreach → Product Launch Plan, Marketing Plan

Acquire — Thought Leadership, Customer Learning, Funnel Optimization, Keeping Existing Customers → Results Tracking, References & Referrals

Sell — Product Sales Process → Mktg / Cust Content, Product Sales Tools, Channel Coaching

Position — Presentations & Demos, Event Delivery, Partner Support, Custom Sales Support

Prepare · Planning · Doing · Deliver

Your 7-step system for transforming any product into a runaway market success.

www.BlueElephantConsulting.com
813.418.6970

Blue Elephant Consulting

v3.0

The **$TOMP** product management system has been created by **Blue Elephant Consulting** to help product managers know what to do and when to do it in order for a product to be successful.

13

Chapter 1

How Yahoo Product Managers Are Kicking Google's Butt

Chapter 1: How Yahoo Product Managers Are Kicking Google's Butt

If you had the choice of being a product manager at either Yahoo or Google, which company would you choose? I'm going to go out on a limb and say that most of us would choose to work at **Google**.

The press is filled with glowing stories about how great everything that Google touches is. Of course, there's the **free food at work** angle also. Likewise, Yahoo has been getting savaged in the press as they lose visitors, botch marketing agreements with Microsoft, and generally drop the ball.

However, it turns out that we might be making the wrong decision. In the battle for capturing viewers for financial information, the Yahoo product managers are **winning the battle** hands down…

Statistics Don't Lie

Randall Stross over at the New York Times has taken a close look the ongoing battle between Google and Yahoo for Web users who are looking for timely financial news. You might think that things are close or that Google is coming on strong. You'd be wrong. Right now Yahoo's financial site is attracting **17.5x the traffic** that Google's financial site is getting. You read that correctly: not 2x, not 10x, but 17.5x!

This is not a recent occurrence either. For the last **19 months** (1.6 years if you care) Yahoo Finance has been #1 in this category. Google is currently ranked 17th. Yahoo was able to attract 21.7M unique visitors while Google has only been able to attract 1.2M unique visitors.

What Yahoo Product Managers Are Doing Right

In talking with Yahoo's product managers, Stross found that they had taken the time to sit down with their target audience and discover what they wanted – and what they didn't want. This research revealed that the more financial information that was presented to users, the **greater their anxiety became**.

Once the Yahoo product team had this break-through realization, they went ahead and took a page out of Apple's product playbook and created a very simple design that had a clean look that **didn't overload** the visitor with too much information.

The Yahoo team also realized that one of their greatest assets was **other Yahoo sites**. The Yahoo Finance team developed a great relationship with the Yahoo's front page team and they have worked together to identify what topics the Finance team could cover that would allow the front page team to send traffic to them.

Yahoo has achieved this product success with very little original content. In fact, only about 5% of the Yahoo Finance site's information is original. Yahoo realizes that this is a weakness and they plan on boosting this to 10% in the future.

Does Google Have The Better Product?

Does anyone remember the VHS vs. Beta video tape format wars that happened so many years ago? It sure looks like we are looking at a repeat of this once again. Google arguably has a **technically superior financial site.**

Goggle's strategy so far has been to offer visitors the **best financial data and charts**. In the case that this is not enough, Google comes back and offers them even more data and charts.

One of the biggest drawbacks that the Google Finance team has is that Google's home page **does not have a clear link** to the Google Finance page. It's entirely possible that a visitor to the Google home page may never learn that the Google Finance page even exists because the only reference to it is buried in a list of menu items.

One clear advantage that Google has over the Yahoo Finance page is that they offer **free real-time price quotations** obtained directly from the New York Stock Exchange and NASDAQ. Yahoo Finance on the other hand gets its stock prices from the BATS Exchange and they have a delay of roughly 1 minute.

Google visitors get real-time stock prices for free, Yahoo visitors **have to pay** for access to real-time quotes – $10.95 or $13.95 / month (NYSE or NASDAQ).

Final Thoughts

Who's going to win this battle? You would think that that with Google's deep pockets they would eventually come out the victor. However, it appears as though Google's product managers **still don't get it**.

A case in point is Google's new set of stock price charting tools that they call "**Technicals**". These tools allow users to analyze stock prices over time using 12 different technical formulas. Based on what Yahoo has discovered about visitors to financial information pages, this new set of features will not boost Google's draw.

In the end, the product managers at Yahoo Finance understand that the best way for a free financial site to prosper is by including less mathematics and **more entertainment**. The winner of this battle will inform their users just enough to answer their questions without causing them any unnecessary anxiety.

Product managers at Yahoo who are able to stay tuned into what their finance customers are really looking for will have found yet another way that great product managers make their product(s) **fantastically successful**.

Chapter 2

PayPal Product Managers Try To Win a Popularity Contest

Chapter 2: PayPal Product Managers Try To Win a Popularity Contest

You would think that if your product was the biggest one in its market, you'd be sitting pretty as a product manager, right? Sure, this might be an easy trap to fall into; however, if you start to take it easy once you are the king of the hill, then that's when your competition shows up and knocks you off. Over at the big online payment processor PayPal, their product managers are currently doing quite well. However, they can see **the handwriting on the wall** and are taking some bold steps to remain #1...

What Me Worry?

If you want to have a successful product that everyone needs, then the world of **online payment processing** was the business to go into awhile back. Something like a zillion dollars gets exchanged online every day and right now there's pretty much one main player in this industry: eBay's PayPal unit.

As product managers we all realize that when you become very successful, that is a signal for other companies to **create products to compete with you**. It's taken awhile, but now the PayPal product managers are starting to see some serious competition. This is when product managers need to be extra careful and not make marketing mistakes.

And In This Corner We Have...

Don't get me wrong, the PayPal product managers have created a very good product and they've listened to their customers and they've made it very easy to use. However, this market is **too big right now** and growing too fast not to attract some highly qualified competition.

Amazon.com currently sells just about everything on the planet. Amazon.com already has a huge customer base and **enormous computing power**. They are looking to leverage this with a new transaction processing service that they are calling "Pay-Phrase". The Amazon.com product managers are betting that if they make it even easier to shop with them, then more people will do so.

Google offers the most direct competition in their "Google Checkout" payment processing system. One of their greatest strengths going forward is that this service has been integrated into the **Android mobile operating system**.

Facebook may represent the greatest threat to the PayPal product manager's long term success. Simply put, Facebook's user base of over **300 million users** gives it an unprecedented reach into the consumer market. This is exactly what any online payment processing company needs in order to succeed.

The Facebook product managers have created a virtual currency called Facebook Credits that can be used to buy both virtual and real goods. Right now only a few vendors are using these credits to allow users to buy things, but that may all change quickly. Facebook has opened up **a gift shop** that accepts Facebook credits and they are starting to sell both virtual goods as well as products from other companies. This sure sounds like what they talked about in that book The Innovator's Dilemma...

How PayPal Product Managers Are Fighting Back

As you might expect, the PayPal product managers are not taking this competitive challenge lying down. They believe that the key to their long-term success is to make their payment processing system an **integral part** of many different products so that it will always be there ready to be used by consumers.

In order to make this happen, they are preparing to rollout **a new system** that will make it easier for software developers to integrate the PayPal system into their own applications. This new software, called PayPal X.

The key goal of this new software is to eliminate the need for customers to have to sign into a separate PayPal web site in order to complete their purchase. Instead, they'll be able to complete it **without leaving the web site that they are on**.

What All of This Means for You

All product managers dream of being responsible for a wildly successful product. The PayPal product managers have clearly succeeded in achieving this dream. What is interesting for the rest of us to observe is what they do now: do they rest on their laurels or **do they kept moving forward?**

Clearly PayPal's competition has shown up in force in the guise of both Amazon.com and Facebook. Both of these companies have the luxury of having been able to watch what PayPal has done and learning from their mistakes. The products that the competition rolls out will pose a serious threat to PayPal.

Before you start feeling too sorry for those poor successful PayPal product managers, realize that they seem to **have realized** that they are facing a threat and are taking steps to stay in the lead.

For the rest of us, I believe that the message from this competition needs to be that no matter how successful our product becomes, **we can never take it easy**. We will always have competition, it's what we do to meet it is what determines how successful we will be as product managers.

Chapter 3

Is Dancing With Yourself Wrong For Product Mangers To Do?

Chapter 3: Is Dancing With Yourself Wrong For Product Mangers To Do?

What's a product manager to do when your #1 competitor is **your own product?** What can you do if you spend a lot of time and money developing a new version of your product and then roll it out and the customers that you want to sell it to appear to be happy using the old version of your product? This is exactly the situation that Microsoft's Office product managers now find themselves in...

Done In By Their Own Success

Everybody knows what Microsoft's Office product is, don't you? It's the **premier suite of business software tools** that just about everybody uses everyday (this article is being written in Microsoft Word). The very fact that it's so popular is what creates such a challenge for its product mangers.

Office 2010 is the next version that is getting ready to be rolled out. It's got a bunch of fancy **new features** that are going to permit people to simultaneously work on documents, link into Facebook, etc. But are people going to buy it?

Over at the research company Gartner Inc., they've done some interesting studies on just **how many people have been willing to upgrade** their perfectly good versions of Office to a new version in the past. Only 60% of current Office users bothered to upgrade to Office 2003 when it came out. When Office 2007 came out, somewhere between 50-55% of users upgraded to it. I wonder how things will go for Office 2010?

Why Not Just Go Ahead And Upgrade?

As product managers, we can get very close to our products. Maybe too close. When we roll out a new version of an existing product, we can fool ourselves into thinking that all of our existing customers will of course want to upgrade to it because it has so many **cool new features**. But that's just the problem; they are features, not benefits.

What we too quickly overlook is that from our customer's point-of-view, any upgrade is a **pain in the butt**. There are a lot of hassles and expenses involved. Sure there is the cost of the new product (didn't I already pay for this?) but then there is also the retraining that is involved. Once a customer takes into account just how large their user base is, both of these disruptions can quickly become too much to put up with.

Uh, Oh — Microsoft Is Late To the Party

Oh, there's one more thing that the Microsoft product managers have to worry about. As you can well imagine, past versions of the Office product don't do everything that customers want. Well guess what: a bunch of companies have seen this market opportunity and have **dived right in**.

Small start-ups that are run by former Microsoft employees have created tools that can be added to existing versions of Office that provide many of the **key new features** that Office 2010 will provide — without the hassle of upgrading. Some of these firms are Xobni (email search), DocVerse (collaboratively edit documents over the Internet), Gist (interface email to social networking sites), and Xiant (helps to file email more efficiently).

This, of course, makes life even more difficult for Microsoft's Office product managers. Why should existing customers upgrade if they can already get the new product's **key new functionality** simply by adding free or low cost plugins to their existing software?

What All of This Means for You

The Microsoft Office product managers have a challenge on their hands. They have a very successful product; however, now they have a new version of the product and they want as many of their existing customers to decide that the expense and hassle of upgrading is **worth the effort**.

Just to make things even more difficult, an entire industry has sprung up creating add on products that **eliminate** some of the most obvious customer pain points that Microsoft could normally use to motivate customers to upgrade. This limits Microsoft's options.

What should be most important for product managers everywhere is that **Microsoft has deep pockets** and they realize that they have a problem here. I suspect that we're going to seem a full out push to motivate customers to upgrade: advertising, pricing, and incentives will all be used. We should all take careful notes and learn what works so that we can use it the next time we upgrade our product...

Chapter 4

Case Study: What To Do When A Large Competitor Shows Up On Your Block

Chapter 4: Case Study: What to Do When a Large Competitor Shows Up On Your Block

There's not a product manager out there who doesn't dream of the day in which their product is the **only show in town**. Man – wouldn't that be great? You wouldn't have to worry about any real competition; you'd just be spending your time working to grow the market. And then you wake up.

The new-kid-on-the-block firm Redbox who has taken the DVD rental market by storm with their low-price, limited selection kiosks that have been popping up everywhere. For the longest time it looked like it would be a Redbox vs. Netflix battle. However, **things have changed**.

There's a new gorilla in town: NCR. Just a little while ago NCR purchased Houston-based TNR Holdings which was a smaller player, but they were in the kiosk DVD rental business also. This wouldn't be all that remarkable if the product managers at NCR hadn't done something else interesting: **gotten into bed with Blockbuster**.

The NCR product managers have somehow talked Blockbuster into licensing its brand to NCR. This allows Blockbuster to take a cut of rental revenue from the kiosks. Hmm, I had sort of thought that Netflix had Blockbuster on the ropes. Is this a way for the Blockbuster product managers to **stage a rebound** ("don't call it a comeback")?

What Does This Mean For Redbox?

As though things weren't heating up enough for the Redbox product managers, the latest news is that NCR is acquiring DVD Kiosk operator DVDPlay Inc. and plans on converting its **1,300 kiosks** to the Blockbuster Express brand name. Now we're starting to talk about a lot of kiosks.

What makes this latest purchase by NCR even more interesting is that it will give NCR a leg up in one of Redbox's weakest markets: California. As product managers are all too painfully aware, it's a lot harder to boost your product's market share when you have to **take market away from your competition!**

That deal that the NCR product managers struck with Blockbuster seems to be paying off. NCR is reporting that converting kiosks to the Blockbuster brand appears to **boost their traffic significantly.** Think about it, would you rent a DVD from NCR? No way; however, when you see the Blockbuster name and the blue and gold colors you start to think about Friday nights and relaxing at home in front of the TV.

Remember, the key to this product's success is **volume.** The kiosks rent out movies for as little as $1 per night. In order to boost their volume so that they can compete with Redbox better, as NCR replaces the DVDPlay kiosks with the Blockbuster kiosks, they plan on moving them to better locations. Some of these locations include moving them outside of stores so that people can still access them even when the store is closed.

The 900 lb. Gorilla in the Room

Gosh, you're thinking, it looks like the Redbox product managers now have their hands full. Wait a minute, **it gets even more complicated.** Redbox's low-price marketing strategy has been so successful that some studios try to keep their newest releases out of kiosks to avoid devaluing the same products that they are trying to sell in stores for $30.

Kiosks operators like Redbox have been trying to get around this problem by **buying DVDs in quantity** from either Walmart or Best Buy. The bad news is retailers have caught on to this strategy and are now putting restrictions on how many DVDs kiosk operators can purchase. In some cases they are restricting purchases to just three of any single title.

Redbox has **antitrust suits** pending against Twentieth-Century Fox, Warner Bros., and Universal Pictures.

New Competition Is Arriving Every Day

As though having competition from a large firm with deep pockets that has gotten into bed with one of your biggest established competitors wasn't enough, there are **other startup firms** that Redbox still has to worry about.

Mosquito Productions has a BigBox DVD kiosk that contains between **2,000 – 3,000 DVDs** compared to 500 for Redbox and 950 for Blockbuster Express.

In a business with very low barriers to entry, Redbox needs to anticipate that there will be **even more firms** like this showing up over time.

What All of This Means for You

What the Redbox product managers are going through should **serve as an example for all of us**. It's great to be one of the first entrants into a new market and to be successful for a while. However, we all have to remember that success is like blood in the water and it will attract other sharks soon enough.

Once competition heats up product managers need to shift some of their focus from growing their market share to **holding on to what they already have**. This means that they need to find ways to differentiate their product.

This might be a great time for Redbox to start to develop a **"frequent renter"** program in order to allow customers to build up "credits". This could help customers decide to choose a Redbox kiosk over any others when they have a choice.

Chapter 5

Is Being Yellow The Worst Product Management Job In The World – Or Not?

Chapter 5: Is Being Yellow The Worst Product Management Job In The World – Or Not?

When I was first out living on my own, the arrival of the latest copy of the yellow (and white) pages was **a big deal**. Since my parents had always received these huge volumes, when I got mine I felt that somehow I was now a "grown up". Fast forward to the 21st Century and man have things changed. There still are Yellow Pages®, but is it possible that owning this product is the worst product management job ever?

What Happened To the Yellow Pages?

Once upon a time the Yellow Pages **ruled the world of local search**. Everybody in the U.S. had a phone and we all got service from the same phone company, AT&T, so it was simple for AT&T to create a Yellow Pages product and drop it off on the doorstep of each one of their existing customers.

Then things started to get weird. AT&T got broken up by a Federal judge. All of a sudden, we still had AT&T, but we also had 7 local new companies that provided local telephone service. There was also a bunch of new guys who were starting to also provide local phone service. What this meant is that if you had a phone, then you started to get multiple Yellow Pages-like books dropped off on your doorstep.

Just to make things even more complicated, the online world started to explode. This meant that the stronger local providers could start to push their **online equivalents of the Yellow Pages** such as SuperPages.com (offered by Verizon). In case that didn't confuse you enough, both Yahoo and Google started to customize the results that people started to get when they'd do searches for local businesses.

What a Yellow Pages Product Manager Could Be Doing

Pity the poor Yellow Pages product manager. Once upon a time he/she was king/queen of the hill in the kingdom of local search. However, now they are **just another player** and they keep finding themselves losing ground to the new entrants (when you own a market, what else can happen to you?)

The local search marketing agency TMP Directional Marketing | 15miles, did a study of how consumers were searching for information on local businesses. What they found was that in the 3 years from 2007-2009 consumers reported that their use of the print version of the Yellow Pages to find a local business **went down by 5%**. This was coupled with 71% of consumers reporting that they use the print version of the Yellow Pages less than once a week.

So what's a print Yellow Pages product manager to do? I believe that this is one of those marketing conditions that screams out for **"out of the box thinking"**. Here are three ideas for what Yellow Pages product managers could do:

- **Syndicate:** What this means is that when a local business agrees to place an ad with the Yellow Pages, make sure that that ad starts to show up in more places than just the printed book that gets dropped off at people's houses. Dare I say that the Yellow Pages need to become a portal? Instead come up with a way to offer local discounts and promote a vendor-of-the-day, etc.

- **Go Mobile:** Let's face it, who wants to take the time to find their printed copy of the Yellow Pages let alone open it up and try to find what you are looking for when you can do the same thing quicker on your mobile phone? The Yellow Pages needs to come up with a local search "app" that everyone instinctively uses when they want to find a local business.

- **Get Social:** Give it up – Facebook is here to stay. There has to be a Yellow Pages angle to all of the social networking that everyone is doing. Yellow Pages product managers need to become the conduit between their advertisers and the local customers who are using everything from Facebook to Twitter.

What All of This Means for You

Don't laugh at the Yellow Pages product managers too loudly – you could be **in a similar situation** with your product some day in the future. What we need to do is to understand how they got into this situation and what they are doing to get out of it.

The Yellow Pages is a product that competes in a market segment called **"local search"**. Once upon a time, the big Yellow Pages book that got dropped off at everyone's house owned this market. Now new competitors such as Google Maps have taken the lion's share of the market away from the Yellow Pages.

Yellow Pages product managers need to be willing to change with **the changes in their market**. This means that they need to find ways to have their product be effective in multiple channels. Additionally they will need to move aggressively into new media areas such as mobile devices in order to remain relevant.

Being a Yellow Pages product manager is not an easy job. However, if you really wanted to go to work every day and face a challenge that would allow you **to make a difference**, then perhaps the Yellow Pages is the place to be!

Chapter 6

What a Video Rental Store Can Teach Product Managers

Chapter 6: What a Video Rental Store Can Teach Product Managers

Not to date myself or anything, but can anyone else remember going to the video store on a Friday or Saturday night? I'd wander the aisles and take a look at every movie on the "just released" rack in order to decide which one or two videos I was going to rent. Netflix and the Internet have pretty much **killed the video store** these days and so what's a video store product manager to do?

(Streaming) Video Killed the Video Store

To be a video store product manager in the 1990s was the bomb! Everyone finally had a VCR in their house and the movie studios were cranking out movies, both new and old, on video tape left and right. Your only real problem was trying to **get your stock level right** so that you could meet the needs of most of your customers.

Almost overnight everything changed. Those darn DVDs came along. Sure, you could start to replace the tapes in your stores with DVDs, but all of a sudden the product managers over at Netflix discovered that you could cheaply use the U.S. postal mail to **send DVDs to people's homes**. Oh, oh – now your video store was under threat. There was nothing in anyone's product manager job description that told them how to handle this situation.

As though things couldn't get even worse, they did. Since so many consumers now had high-speed internet service to their house, the Netflix product managers moved on to the next stage of their game: **offering streaming video** and making it so you didn't even have to wait by your mailbox anymore.

Given all of these superior ways to get your hands on the latest and greatest videos, why would anyone still make the trek to the video store and run the risk of **incurring late fees**? There are some people for whom a weekend video is still a spur-of-the-moment purchase. These last remaining people were vacuumed up when the product managers from Redbox placed their self-service DVD rental kiosks outside of 7-11's and other stores. That's it, game over for the video stores.

How Video Stores Are Being Reborn

But wait, all of the video stores have not gone away. Sure, sure – the big chain ones like Blockbuster and Hollywood Video have been closing their doors left and right. However, a number of **the independent video stores** are still open for business. What have their product managers been doing?

A number of the video stores have **changed the products that they offer to their customers**. Some have started to offer events. Nicole LaPorte from the New York Times reports that these have included a film studies program, classes on anime mythology, lectures by filmmakers and spoken word events. Clearly, this isn't your father's Blockbuster store.

What you're starting to see is that place that we used to go to rent video tapes is transforming itself into more of a community gathering place or a cultural hub for people who really like films. The video store product managers are positioning their products to be **different than Netflix** which clearly has no soul: it is both nameless (who is sending me those videos?) and faceless (exactly where is Netflix located?).

Video Store 2.0

All of this **"connect with your customers"** strategic management stuff is good short-term product manager positioning. However, what should video store product managers be doing in order to prepare for the long-term?

Dr. Peter Fader is a very smart marketing professor at the University of Pennsylvania who thinks that he knows the answer. Here's the most important point that he makes: as easy as it would be to do, video stores that want to survive must not consider Netflix as **an adversary**. Netflix is just too easy to use and if you position them as the enemy, then you'll force your customers to choose and in the long run the video store will lose.

Dr. Fader has a different suggestion. He believes that video stores should position themselves as **an alternative to Netflix**. Yes, when people want to watch the summer's latest action flick, they'll turn to Netflix. However, when they want a film that might not be in the mainstream, one that is a bit harder to find and which Netflix doesn't have, that's when the video store can step in.

The video stores' current efforts to provide film based events at the store are another great way to **supplement what their customers are getting from Netflix**. Instead of thinking of video customers as having to pick either Netflix or the local video store, instead start to think of the video store as just being a part of a video watcher's portfolio of video information sources. This is the path to a video store's long-term success.

What All of This Means for You

As product managers, we all seem to spend our time trying to figure out how we can make our products more successful. We scheme and plan ways to capture another 1% of market share. What we rarely spend any time thinking about is the very real possibility that one day **our whole market might just vanish**.

Video stores had this happen to them with the arrival of Netflix and Redbox. The video stores that didn't adapt are now gone. The ones that realized what was happening and who **have transformed themselves** are still here. In order to survive in the long run, these stores are going to have to create an entirely new market for themselves and find a way to coexist with the new video delivery services.

Product managers should learn from this story that **the game is never over** even when your account manager or business development manager starts to panic. The rules might change, the players might change, and how we keep score may be done differently. However, as long as you have the ability to roll with the punches, your product can deal with almost any change that comes along and you'll emerge on the other side stronger and better for the adventure. Now put that on your product manager resume!

Chapter 7

Why Product Managers Need To Learn To Love Being #2

Chapter 7: Why Product Managers Need To Learn To Love Being #2

If you're a product manager, then **you always want to be a winner, right?** It's almost an integral part of our product development definition — you want your product to storm into the marketplace and kick some butt and become #1 overnight. You want to climb to the top of your marketplace and you want to stay there forever. Sounds simple, doesn't it? You'd be right if it weren't for the fact that sometimes you'll be more successful if your product is #2...

The Problem with Becoming #1

Yes, becoming #1 sure seems like a great thing to do. Look at Apple's iPhone; look at Google's search product. We all know that these products are #1 and that they are **very, very successful**. That's the kind of story that every product manager wants to add to his or her product manager resume

However, what we're missing here is that it's very expensive in terms of both time and effort to become #1. Also, there's the downside in that once you become #1, everyone else in your market starts to try to take your position over – **you have become a target.**

The other challenge with becoming #1 is that **nobody ever stays #1 for long** – it's always a temporary position. This was the challenge that I faced recently when I was working with one of my customers who sells products in the telecommunications space.

They had just developed a new product that promised to provide the fastest service to a very specific segment of their market. They were very excited about this new product and they wanted my help in determining how they could go to market with it in order to **gain the most market share**.

The problem that I quickly identified was that the customers that they wanted to go after **had already solved the problem that their product addressed**. These potential customers had needed a solution and so they had gone with the only solution that was available to them – which just happened to be offered by my customer's competition.

The majority of the potential customers for this product were now **locked up** into multi-year contracts and there really were not that many customers available to buy my customer's new product no matter how great it was. Talk about a product management problem!

Why Being #2 Is Sometimes Better

The more that I looked into my customer's problem, the more that I realized that the end customer for their product was actually spending a lot more money on a solution than we had originally realized. It turns out that yes; they had solved their initial problem by selecting a competing product. However, **they were required to also have a back-up communication path** just in case something happened to their primary solution.

What this meant is that they were spending a lot of money to stitch together a second solution. Ah ha – **an idea was born**.

I sat down with some potential customers and discovered that they were **eager to find a better solution** for their backup solution. The way that they had solved this issue was not elegant and they weren't very happy with it. Clearly this was a market that was waiting to be tapped.

You might think that that was the end of the story, but it wasn't. My customer **had a hard time with this idea**. They were very, very proud of their product and they really wanted to go to market with a big splash and become #1. I think at one time or another we've all felt this way.

I ended up sitting down with them and having a long talk with them. The concept was simple, the explaining took some time. I pointed out that capturing a part of the "I'm #1" market would be good, but it might be a struggle to make and keep their product profitable. However, there was a real opportunity for them to capture **the lion's share** of the backup connection market and nobody else would be competing with them for that.

When you are #2, you generally have to price your product lower than the company at #1 does. However, there is a real good chance that you'll be able to **sell a lot more of your product** and this means that your product could end up making a lot more money than the #1 product. In the end, isn't that why we do what we do?

What All of This Means for You

Everybody likes to be #1 and product managers are no exception to this rule. We'd all like to think that being #1 is a part of our product manager job description. However, sometimes we need to pause for a moment and **determine if being #1 is really the best thing for our product**.

When a product manager focuses on making their product #1, then it takes a lot of time and energy to get there. Assuming that it's even possible, once you become #1 it can be very difficult to **hold on to that title** when there are so many competitors trying to steal your crown from you.

An alternative is to shoot for the #2 spot. This can be a much less contested position for a product. Additionally, it may turn out to be **more profitable for your product** because the available market may be several times larger for you.

Product managers always have to consider what's best for our product. Sometimes **our own ego can get in the way** – we all want to be #1. Next time you have an opportunity to consider where you want your product to fit into a market, give the #2 spot a consideration – it might be a perfect fit...!

Chapter 8

To Beat the Competition, Product Managers Have To Do Some Homework

Chapter 8: To Beat the Competition, Product Managers Have To Do Some Homework

Based on the product development definition that you used to create your product, your product is the best available product to solve the problem that your customers are facing. This means that your customers should all be buying from you and your competition should just dry up and blow away, right? For some odd reason, that does not seem to be happening. Product managers who want their products to beat the competition need to do some homework in order to **find out just exactly what their competition is up to...**

How Much Is Your Competition Selling?

This one's pretty simple, isn't it? In order to determine just how much of a competitor a firm is, you're going to have to find out **how successful their product is** — this is basic product manager resume stuff. This means that you've got some sales numbers that you've got to uncover.

I'm sure that we all know that getting this information is valuable. However, do we understand why? One of the most important reasons that we need to understand how successful our competition is comes down to the simple fact that it will help us to **set our own expectations for our product**. At the same time, it will expose potential market opportunities; reveal possible partners, and might even let us know about threats that we had not realized existed.

Getting the sales information that we need may not be easy especially if your competition is not a publically traded firm. However, there are always ways around this. One such way is to go to trade groups or industry publications to get information on the size of your product's market. Then see if you can get analyst's estimates of **the portion of the market that your**

competition has captured. If they have 20% of a US$100M market, then you know that they're selling $20M worth of product each year.

How Much Does Your Competition Pay Their Employees?

In order to design, develop, market, and sell their product, your competition needs workers. As we all know, there will always be turn over when it comes to employees. This means that your competition is always going to have "help wanted" ads running. **These are ads that you need to be spending some time reading**.

These ads are going to tell you a lot about **how your competition is running their business**. One of the most important things that you can learn is how much they are willing to pay their staff. Since you'll be needing the same types of workers for your product, if you know how much the competition is willing to pay, then you can raise your salaries just a bit an you'll be able to land the very best employees.

Nothing Beats Talking To Real People

Google is a very powerful tool when it comes to finding out what your competition is up to. However, there are **even better ways** to get good information.

Simply by **talking with your competition**, you can often learn a great deal about not only their product, but also how they are going about selling their product. This is the kind of information that you'll never get out of Google.

However, you need to realize that you are operating in dangerous territory here. **You can never misrepresent yourself**. I am going to suggest that you always identify who you are and who you work for when you are talking with your competition. You'll be amazed at just how much they are willing to share with you even when they know who you are!

What All of This Means for You

In order for your product to be successful, you are going to have to **acknowledge that you will have competition**. This means that you've got some homework to do: you need to find out as much about your competition as possible. This kind of work should have been spelled out in your product manager job description.

In order to do this, you can **use many freely available resources**. This should allow you to determine just how much of the available market your competition has been able to capture. It should also let you find out how much they are paying their employees and what kind of benefits they are providing. Finally, you need to keep in mind that going out and talking with real people is always your best way of collecting valuable information about your competition.

It can be too easy for a product manager to spend their time only looking inside of their own company. We can get caught up in our product development process and interacting with our own sales teams. Take the time to **do your homework** and you'll learn more about your market. Your competition is being successful, study what they are doing and your product can become successful also!

Chapter 9

When Competitors Merge: What Three Things Should A Product Manager Do?

Chapter 9: When Competitors Merge: What Three Things Should A Product Manager Do?

Sometimes as product managers we wish that our lives could become better if only one of our competitors would just go away. It's events that like this that would make developing your product development definition just a bit easier. Somewhat amazingly this does happen. However, all too often, the reason that they went away was because **they were bought by one of our other competitors**. This means that we now have a new much larger competitor to deal with. What's a product manager to do?

What You Should Probably Not Do

When two of your competitors combine to create a new single larger competitor, almost every product manager has the same initial reaction: **"we need to do that"**. The thinking is that by acquiring another firm, your company will be able to match your new competitor.

However, Thomas Keil and Tomi Laamanen, researchers who have studied such events, caution us that all too often reacting that way **is not in our long-term best interests**. What they found is that companies who did their own merger after competitors merged seemed to end up doing more poorly than everyone else and that's not going to look good on your product manager resume.

There were **three reasons for this**. The first is that any decision made under pressure is often going to be the wrong decision. The next is that the cost of any remaining firms will go up after the first merger is announced. Finally, the first firm got the pick of the litter and the firms that are left may not be as good.

Alternative Responses Product Managers Should Consider

So if your gut reaction is wrong, then what course of action is a product manager to suggest when your CEO comes to you and asks you what the company should do after your competitors have merged? The good news is that there are **three different courses of action** that you can take that just might put your product in a more competitive position:

- **Retreat!:** If all of this merging is happening in a non-primary market for your product, consider pulling out. Since it is now going to take more time and effort to compete with a larger competitor, it might be in your best interest to pull back and focus on only those markets where you know that you can dominate and be successful.

- **Take A Step To The Left:** Instead of responding to the merger of rivals with a merger of your own, instead focus on growing your product by both innovation and organic growth. Let's face it, no merger goes smoothly. Both of your competitors who merged are going to be distracted by the effort of trying to combine two different companies for some time. Use this time to find ways to make your product even better and you'll come out ahead over time.

- **Start Small:** Instead of recommending that your company go out and buy a company of equal size to the one that your competition bought, instead take a "smaller is better" approach. Identify a series of smaller companies that if purchased by your company will eventually yield the same result as if you had paid much more to buy a single larger company.

What Does All of This Means for You

Managing a product means **living in a dynamic environment** even if this was never spelled out that way in your product manager job description. Sometimes our competition makes our lives more difficult by merging and then presenting us with fewer, but stronger, competitors.

When this happens product managers need to resist the gut instinct that makes them want to recommend that their company **merge with another company**. Instead, alternate responses such as retreating, maneuvering, or alternate acquisitions may be the right response.

When changes happen the worst thing that you can do is to **react too quickly**. Instead, take the time and think about your end game: what do you really want to happen. Once you know what that is, take the time to do the right thing to make it happen. Product managers who know how to correctly react to a merger of competitors will end up being the most successful.

Chapter 10

How Product Managers Should Go About Doing Business Research

Chapter 10: How Product Managers Should Go About Doing Business Research

In order for your product to be successful, you are going to have to have to have **a good understanding of your market**. I wish that I could tell you that there was some sort of pill or potion that you could take that would magically provide you with the information that you need. Sorry, such a quick solution does not currently exist. Instead, you're going to have to do some business research on your market. Do you know how to go about doing that?

Business Research: The Process

The good news about doing business research is that the best way to go about doing it is **as part of a process** that if mastered, can go on your product manager resume. The purpose of the process is to provide you with a way to make sure that you are able to both collect and process all of the information that you're going to need in order to become a market expert.

The first step in the process of doing business research is to **collect the basic data that you'll need**. This is done using a combination of data from both primary sources (from customers) and secondary sources (from other sources). Ideally you want to get as much information from your customers as possible; however, getting information about your market from other sources will also provide you with value.

The next step is to transform the data that you've collected into **useful information**. Generally speaking, you'll start out with a lot of data and you'll process it and end up with a smaller amount of information. Often times generating information can be as simple as organizing the data that you already have.

Given that you now have information on your market, you now need to **reach agreement with other people in your company** as to what the information means. This is an opportunity to work in other pieces of information about your market that may have been collected by other parts of the company.

Information by itself will be of little use to you. You need to understand how that information can be used to predict what will happen in your market going forward. That's where **a model of the market comes in**. You'll want to take the information that you have, plug it into your model and then take a look at the predictions that the model produces.

The final step in your business research process is for you to make decisions based on what your market model tells you. You must keep in mind that your decisions will then **impact the model** so you'll have to go back and add your decisions to the model in order to keep it up-to-date.

The #1 Business Research Challenge

Great, you've got an assignment: do some business research and you've got a process. As a product manager **you should be all taken care of, right?** Well, it turns out that this is not the case. There is one step in the process that always seems to take more time than it should.

This would be the part where you **get agreement from the rest of your company** as to what the information that you've been able to create from your collected data actually means. You would think that you'd be dealing with a collection of facts that everyone could agree on, but more often than not this is not the case. Getting this type of agreement was never part of your product manager job description.

What happens is your information may indicate that a new company is becoming a serious competitor. However, the people in your sales organization may not agree with you. This is the kind of thing that can lead to **very long discussions and disagreements**. How these issues get resolved is critical because this is the information that is eventually going to be used to make product decisions.

What All of This Means for You

Before you create a product development definition, design a marketing plan, or even start to think about what is going to have to go into your product's launch plan, **first you need to understand your market**. The best way to go about doing this is to do some business research.

Business research is simply a process by which you discover **how your market operates**. The business research process consists of collecting data about your market segment, transforming that data into actionable information, getting internal agreement about what the information means, using tools to process the information, and then making the decisions that will impact your product. Getting agreement on just what facts relate to your product may turn out to be the most difficult part of the process.

Within most companies the product manager is the one person that anyone who has a question about the product or the market can come to. In order to **be able to answer all of the questions that you'll be asked**, make sure that you've done the business research that is needed to have the right answers to their questions.

Chapter 11

Product Managers Who Spy On the Competition

Chapter 11: Product Managers Who Spy On the Competition

What do your customers think about your product? Do they like it better than your competition's product? Did you do a good job when you created your product development definition? Would it be helpful to you **to know more about your competition's product?** I'm willing to bet that the answer to this question is "yes". Now the big questions is just exactly how can a product manager go about getting the competitive intelligence about a competitor that you need?

Know Your Competition

This seems like a silly step, right? **Don't we all just automatically know who our product's competition is?** Well, the answer is often no – we think that we do, but we really don't. When was the last time that you sat down and really took a look at your market in order to fully understand who you are competing with? Get good at doing this and you'll have something to add to your product manager resume.

All too often, your product is competing against other firms that **you may not even be aware of**. The best way to determine who your real competition is can be to talk with your customers. Find out who they were considering before they selected your product. This will provide you with a true list of who you are up against.

Sometimes the greatest competition that you are facing may be what is called **an indirect competitive threat**. This is the type of product or service that generally falls outside of what a product manager considers to be your competition. A great example of this would the case of the soft drink Pepsi which we all know competes with Coke, but which it turns out also competes with water.

Know Your Product

Just as awkward as the question about who your competition is, it turns out that there is a question that is even more awkward. **What makes your product so special?** What are your product's strengths?

It turns out that it's going to do you no good to collect competitive intelligence about your competition **if you don't know what your product does well**. What the information that you'll be collecting is designed to do is to expose your competition's weaknesses against your strengths. However, if you don't know what you are good at, then you're not going to be able to do this.

Ultimately this is all going to go back to the strategy that your company is pursuing for your product. **Do you know what this is?** You're going to have to. One of the things that your competitive intelligence gathering efforts are going to have to reveal is your competition's strategy. In order to understand how to compete with them, you'll have to understand your own strategy.

It's All About (Former) Employees

This is where things can get a bit dicey, but some of your best competitive information will probably **come from your competitor's former employees**. This means that you need to establish a system to collect the information about their former employer that they are willing to share with you.

The first way to get information about your competition from former employees is to **take a look at the resumes that your company is receiving** for your open positions from people who have worked for other firms. Take a look at what projects they worked on, what their accomplishments were, and the dates that they did the work. This may reveal to you future products that have not yet been introduced.

Your next step in the competitive information collection process will be to **participate in the interviews** with people who have worked for your competition. Please be very careful to not cause them to violate any nondisclosure agreements. You'll want to see if you can do some probing in order to learn things about the culture at your competitor and why this person decided to leave. This is all good information for you to have!

What All of This Means for You

Our customers always have choices when they are looking for a way to solve a problem. We hope that they'll choose our product, but there is always the possibility that **they'll decide to go with one of our competitor's products**. In order to prevent this from happening, it's a product manager's job to find out as much about his or her competition as possible. Even if this isn't part of your product manager job description, it is something that you'll have to get good at.

Knowing your competition starts with making sure that **you know just exactly who your competition is**. Next, you need to understand what all of your customer's options are for solving their problem. Knowing what strengths your product has will help you to understand exactly who your completion is. Finally, some of the best competitive intelligence will come from your competition's former employees.

If this was a perfect world, **our products would have no competition**. However, it's not and they do. This means that part of your job as a product manager is to find out everything that you can about your competition in order to make sure that customers select your product over theirs. Take the time to do this correctly and you'll be ahead of the game.

Chapter 12

Sensual Product Management: Umm, What Do We Need To Know?

Chapter 12: Sensual Product Management: Umm, What Do We Need To Know?

So there is no delicate way to talk about this topic, but I'm going to bring it up anyway. As product managers, we're often not above **using sex appeal to motivate potential customers to buy our product**. However, what happens if the product that we're trying to sell is sex itself?

Welcome to the World of Cams and "Tips"

Matt Richtel wrote a story for the New York Times talking about this new market where (primarily) women with video cameras are **offering services over the Internet** to (primarily) men. It doesn't take a product development definition to get set up – just a laptop and a video camera. Once these have been secured, the next step is for the women to set up an account on a hub web site such as YourFreeCam or Live Jasmine.

Once that's been taken care of, the women are then free to put on their own one-woman shows. Web surfers can then drop by their video feed. If a surfer likes what they see, then they can **"tip" the model** which transfers money from the surfer's account with the hub site to the model. It appears as though the model gets roughly half of the tip; the hub site keeps the other half.

What caught my attention in Matt's story is that at any time in the day, he reported that **there were over 1,000 of these cam models online**. Wow – talk about competition! If this was a product that you were offering, you'd be hard pressed to distinguish your product offering.

Let's think about this for a minute. You have over 1,000 women all competing for the attention of a limited number of web surfers. You would expect each women to **start to specialize** (fetishes anyone?). However, even if you did that, there could easily be 100+ other women who had decided to specialize in the same area that you had selected. What's a cam model to do?

How You Could Do a Better Job of Marketing Yourself

Although I suspect that none of us are currently working in the cam model business (however, if you are, then welcome), it's **a good product manager exercise** to give some thought about how you'd handle this situation even if you're not going to be adding it to your product manager resume. How could you get more surfers to (1) visit your video feed and (2) tip you more?

The first problem is what is it going to take to get traffic? Step one would be to brand yourself. It probably doesn't matter what name or tag line you use, just pick one – **that will distinguish you** from most of the other 1,000 women that you are competing against.

You will have surfers who will organically drop by your video channel. You need to come up with a way **to get them to stay**, and then to become repeat customers. One way to make this happen would be to "schedule" shows. Tell everyone that something is going to happen on a given date at a given time. When you reach the end of a show, inform your viewers when the next show will be and why they would want to plan on attending. This is almost like what TV shows do with the trailers they have for the next episode.

Finally, you are going to want to **maximize your viewer's tipping**. A great way of making this happen would be to use tipping as a communication vehicle. I believe that tipping levels are shown in real time to the cam models. This means that you could ask your viewers what they wanted you to do: A or B.

Have them tip for A, then have them tip for B, then whichever tip pool turned out to be larger, perform that action. This way your viewers feel involved and you get to keep all of the tips!

What All of This Means for You

Although we may not spend a lot of time thinking about it, one of the most profitable products that the Internet is used to sell is sex in all of its wonderful different forms. The recent arrival of **self-produced cam shows** has opened the door to a flood of new products on this market of Internet sex. The problem is that most of the products all look (pretty much) the same.

From a product manager's point of view this is a market with low barriers to entry, a lot of unbranded suppliers, and customers who can easily switch suppliers. Clearly this would be an undesirable market to enter if only it wasn't such a potentially huge and profitable market. **Product management skills** have to be used to make each performer different from the others. Niche markets have to identified, performers have to create their own brand, and repeat purchases have to be encouraged and rewarded. This is exactly the kind of stuff that shows up in a product manager job description.

No, this may not be the most enjoyable topic to discuss depending on your outlook on life. However, it is clearly a unique market that has a desperate need for **the types of skills that product managers can provide**. As product managers we need to evaluate these types of market conditions in order to improve how we evaluate challenging product management situations and improve our decision making skills.

It's from the forge of failure that the steel of success is formed.

Hard Work Does Not Guarantee Success, But Success Does Not Happen Without Hard Work.

- Dr. Jim Anderson

Create Products Your Customers Want At A Price That They Are Willing To Pay!

Dr. Jim Anderson is available to provide training and coaching on the two topics that are the most important to product managers everywhere: how do I create the products that my customers want and what should I price them at?

Dr. Anderson believes that in order to both learn and remember what he says, product managers need to laugh. Each one of his speeches is full of fun and humor so that what he says "sticks" with everyone.

Dr. Anderson's Product Management Training Includes:

1. How can you segment your market?
2. What problems are your customers having right now?
3. Which of your customer's problems does your product solve?
4. How much of this problem does your product solve?
5. How much will it cost your customer if they don't fix this problem?

Dr. Jim Anderson presents over 100 speeches per year. To invite Dr. Anderson to speak at your event, contact him at:

Phone: 813-418-6970 or
Email: jim@BlueElephantConsulting.com

Blue
Elephant
Consulting
Speaking.   Negotiating.   Managing.   Marketing.

Photo Credits:

Cover - By: Paola Camera
https://www.flickr.com/photos/vegaseddie/

Chapter 1 – By: JD Hancock
https://www.flickr.com/photos/jdhancock/

Chapter 2 – By: Iliveisl
https://www.flickr.com/photos/iliveisl/

Chapter 3 – By: Esparta Palma
https://www.flickr.com/photos/esparta/

Chapter 4 – By: Joe Monin
https://www.flickr.com/photos/jmonin87/

Chapter 5 – By: Thomas Hawk
https://www.flickr.com/photos/thomashawk/

Chapter 6 – By: PJ Mixer
https://www.flickr.com/photos/pjmixer/

Chapter 7 – By: Adam Fagen
https://www.flickr.com/photos/afagen/

Chapter 8 – By: Mark Guitar Photo
https://www.flickr.com/photos/drie0100/

Chapter 9 – By: Craig Taylor
https://www.flickr.com/photos/49333396@N06/

Chapter 10 – By: CCAC North Library
https://www.flickr.com/photos/ccacnorthlib/

Chapter 11 – By: Emory Allen
https://www.flickr.com/photos/ocularinvasion/

Chapter 12 – By: Luke Roberts
https://www.flickr.com/photos/lukeroberts/

Other Books By The Author

Product Management

- How Product Managers Can Grow Their Career: How Product Managers Can Find And Succeed In The Right Job

- Sales Secrets For Product Managers: Tips & Techniques For Product Managers To Better Understand How To Sell Their Product

- Product Management Secrets: Techniques For Product Managers To Boost Product Sales And Increase Customer Satisfaction

- Product Development Lessons For Product Managers: How Product Managers Can Create Successful Products

- Customer Lessons For Product Managers: Techniques For Product Managers To Better Understand What Their Customers Really Want

- Product Failure Lessons For Product Managers: Examples Of Products That Have Failed For Product

Managers To Learn From

- Communication Skills For Product Managers: The Communication Skills That Product Managers Need To Know How To Use In Order To Have A Successful Product

- How To Have A Successful Product Manager Career: The Things That You Need To Be Doing TODAY In Order To Have A Successful Product Manager Career

- Product Manager Product Success: How to keep your product on track and make it become a success

Public Speaking

- How To Become A Better Speaker By Changing How You Speak: Change techniques that will transform a speech into a memorable event

- How To Give A Great Presentation: Presentation techniques that will transform a speech into a memorable event

- How To Rehearse In Order To Give The Perfect Speech: How to effectively rehearse your next speech to that your message be remembered forever!

- Secrets To Creating The Perfect Speech: How to create a speech that will make your message be remembered forever!

- Secrets To Organizing The Perfect Speech: How to organize the best speech of your life!

- Secrets To Planning The Perfect Speech: How to plan to give the best speech of your life

- How To Show What You Mean During A Presentation: How to use visual techniques to transform a speech into a memorable event

CIO Skills

- How CIOs Can Solve The Security Puzzle: Tips And Techniques For CIOs To Use In Order To Secure Both Their IT Department And Their Company

- What CIOs Need To Know About Working With Partners: Techniques For CIOs To Use In Order To Be Able To Successfully Work With Partners

- Critical CIO Management Skills: Decision Making Skills That Every CIO Needs To Have In Order To Be

Able To Make The Right Choices

- How CIOs Can Make Innovation Happen: Tips And Techniques For CIOs To Use In Order To Make Innovation Happen In Their IT Department

- CIO Communication Skills Secrets: Tips And Techniques For CIOs To Use In Order To Become Better Communicators

- Managing Your CIO Career: Steps That CIOs Have To Take In Order To Have A Long And Successful Career

- CIO Business Skills: How CIOs can work effectively with the rest of the company!

IT Manager Skills

- Team Building Strategies For IT Managers: Tips And Techniques That IT Managers Can Use In Order To Develop Productive Teams

- How IT Managers Can Make Innovation Happen: Tips And Techniques For IT Managers To Use In Order To Make Innovation Happen In Their Teams

- Staffing Skills IT Managers Must Have: Tips And Techniques That IT Managers Can Use In Order To

Correctly Staff Their Teams

- Secrets Of Effective Leadership For IT Managers: Tips And Techniques That IT Managers Can Use In Order To Develop Leadership Skills

- IT Manager Career Secrets: Tips And Techniques That IT Managers Can Use In Order To Have A Successful Career

- IT Manager Budgeting Skills: How IT Managers Can Request, Manage, Use, And Track Their Funding

Negotiating

- Learn How To Package Trades In Your Next Negotiation: How To Develop The Skill Of Assembling Potential Trades In Order To Get The Best Possible Outcome

- Learn How To Signal In Your Next Negotiation: How To Develop The Skill Of Effective Signaling In A Negotiation In Order To Get The Best Possible Outcome

- Learn The Skill Of Exploring In A Negotiation: How To Develop The Skill Of Exploring What Is Possible In A Negotiation In Order To Reach The Best

Possible Deal

- Learn How To Argue In Your Next Negotiation: How To Develop The Skill Of Effective Arguing In A Negotiation In Order To Get The Best Possible Outcome

- How To Open Your Next Negotiation: How To Start A Negotiation In Order To Get The Best Possible Outcome

- Preparing For Your Next Negotiation: What You Need To Do BEFORE A Negotiation Starts In Order To Get The Best Possible Deal

- Learn How To Argue In Your Next Negotiation: How To Develop The Skill Of Effective Arguing In A Negotiation In Order To Get The Best Possible Outcome

- How To Open Your Next Negotiation: How To Start A Negotiation In Order To Get The Best Possible Outcome

- Preparing For Your Next Negotiation: What You Need To Do BEFORE A Negotiation Starts In Order To Get The Best Possible Deal

Miscellaneous

- The Internet-Enabled Successful School District Superintendent: How To Use The Internet To Boost Parental Involvement In Your Schools

- Power Distribution Unit (PDU) Secrets: What Everyone Who Works In A Data Center Needs To Know!

- Making The Jump: How To Land Your Dream Job When You Get Out Of College!

"Practical, proven examples of how successful product managers approach competition!"

> This book has been written with one goal in mind – to show you how to use competition to move your product management career forward. We're going to show you how to make sure that this job turns into a success for you!
>
> ## Let's Make Your Career A Success!

What You'll Find Inside:

- **TO BEAT THE COMPETITION, PRODUCT MANAGERS HAVE TO DO SOME HOMEWORK**

- **HOW YAHOO PRODUCT MANAGERS ARE KICKING GOOGLE'S BUTT**

- **CASE STUDY: WHAT TO DO WHEN A LARGE COMPETITOR SHOWS UP ON YOUR BLOCK**

- **HOW PRODUCT MANAGERS SHOULD GO ABOUT DOING BUSINESS RESEARCH**

Dr. Jim Anderson brings his 4 college degrees coupled with over 25 years of real-world experience to this book. He's managed products at some of the world's largest firms as well as at start-ups. He's going to show you what you need to do in order to make your career a success!